California Sea Lion

Fast & Smart!

by Natalie Lunis

Consultants:

Doreen Gurrola, Marine Science Instructor
The Marine Mammal Center, Sausalito, California
www.MarineMammalCenter.org

Jenny Montague, Assistant Curator of Marine Mammals
New England Aquarium, Boston, Massachusetts

BEARPORT
PUBLISHING

NEW YORK, NEW YORK

Credits

Cover, © Mike Scharer/Alamy; TOC, © Franco Banfi/Waterframe/Photolibrary; 4–5, © Masa Ushidoa/SeaPics; 7, © Charles Hood/Oceans Image/Photoshot; 8, Courtesy of Joan Scheier; 9, Courtesy of Joan Scheier; 10, © Phillip Colla/SeaPics; 11, © Norbert Wu/Minden Pictures; 12, © Chijimatsu/e-Photography/SeaPics; 13, © David Wrobel/SeaPics; 14, © Franco Banfi/Waterframe/Photolibrary; 15, © Franco Banfi/Waterframe/Photolibrary; 16T, © Visual & Written/SuperStock; 16B, © Gerard Lacz/NHPA/Photoshot; 17, © Michael S. Nolan/SeaPics; 18T, © Stefan Huwiler/imagebroker/Photolibrary; 18B, © Don Smith/Photodisc/Getty Images; 19, © Shane Thompson/Alamy; 20–21, © Peter Steyn/Ardea; 22, © Phillip Colla/SeaPics; 23TL, © Chijimatsu/e-Photography/SeaPics; 23TR, © janprchal/Shutterstock; 23BL, © Michael S. Nolan/SeaPics; 23BR, © Gerard Soury/Oxford Scientific/Photolibrary.

Publisher: Kenn Goin
Editorial Director: Adam Siegel
Creative Director: Spencer Brinker
Design: Debrah Kaiser
Photo Researcher: Picture Perfect Professionals, LLC

Library of Congress Cataloging-in-Publication Data

Lunis, Natalie.
  California sea lion : fast and smart / by Natalie Lunis.
      p. cm. — (Blink of an eye : superfast animals)
  Includes bibliographical references and index.
  ISBN-13: 978-1-936088-08-9 (library binding)
  ISBN-10: 1-936088-08-8 (library binding)
  1. California sea lion—Juvenile literature. I. Title.
  QL737.P63L86 2011
  599.79'75—dc22
                                    2010017683

For more information, write to Bearport Publishing Company, Inc., 101 Fifth Avenue, Suite 6R, New York, New York 10003. Printed in the United States of America in North Mankato, Minnesota.

072010
042110CGE

10 9 8 7 6 5 4 3 2 1

Contents

A Speedy Swimmer

The California sea lion is one of the fastest animals in the sea.

It can swim at a speed of up to 25 miles per hour (40 kph).

That's five times faster than a swimmer in an Olympic race.

The world's fastest human can swim at a top speed of about 5 miles per hour (8 kph). A gray whale can swim at a top speed of 10 miles per hour (16 kph). A California sea lion can swim faster than both.

Human
5 mph / 8 kph

Gray Whale
10 mph / 16 kph

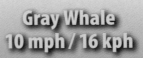

California Sea Lion
25 mph / 40 kph

5

Seals That Roar

The California sea lion is really a kind of seal.

The name "sea lion" comes from the roaring sound that males sometimes make.

Altogether, there are six kinds of sea lions living in the world's oceans. All of them are marine **mammals**, or mammals that live in the sea.

California Sea Lions in the Wild

CANADA

UNITED STATES

California

Pacific Ocean

MEXICO

Atlantic Ocean

■ Where California seal lions live

California sea lions live along a large stretch of the Pacific Coast that includes the coast of California.

male sea lion
roaring

Popular Performers

Many people know California sea lions as smart and playful animals that sometimes do tricks at zoos.

At the Central Park Zoo in New York City, for example, a young sea lion named Clarice has learned to wave at her keepers.

Two other sea lions, Scooter and April, have also learned to signal to their keepers.

They bark at them to call them over at feeding time.

Clarice learning to wave

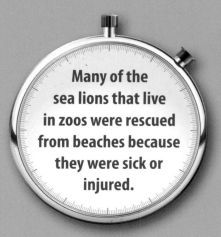

Many of the sea lions that live in zoos were rescued from beaches because they were sick or injured.

In the Wild

How do California sea lions that are living in the wild use their speed and show their cleverness?

They play in the ocean water, tossing seaweed into the air or surfing the waves.

They also swim fast and perform fancy moves for a serious reason—to survive.

They zip through the water to catch food and escape from enemies.

California sea lions are not just powerful swimmers— they are also very graceful. They spin, twirl, and do somersaults as they move underwater.

Swimming Along

California sea lions hunt many kinds of fish, squid, and octopuses.

As they swim after their **prey**, they move their two front **flippers** and two back flippers.

The powerful front flippers move front to back to pull the sea lion through the water.

The back flippers steer its body.

back flippers

front flipper

front flipper

12

squid

Squid are known as very fast swimmers. Some kinds can swim at a top speed of 25 miles per hour (40 kph)—as fast as a sea lion.

13

Diving Down

Usually, California sea lions hunt in shallow waters.

Sometimes, however, they dive down to get food.

They can dive as deep as 1,760 feet (536 m), holding their breath for up to 12 minutes at a time.

The deeper an animal dives, the darker the water around it becomes. When it is hard to see, sea lions use their whiskers to feel the movement of nearby fish and other swimming prey.

whiskers

Escaping from Enemies

Great white sharks and killer whales hunt and eat California sea lions.

Great white sharks catch the sea lions by sneaking up on them.

Killer whales, however, go after them in a high-speed chase.

As the sea lions swim their fastest to get away, they may perform a move called porpoising—jumping out of the water and then diving back in.

great white shark

killer whale

sea lion porpoising

Coming Ashore

California sea lions are built for life both in water and on land.

Using all four flippers, they are able to pull themselves onto sandy or rocky beaches.

Once ashore, they can walk—and even run—on their flippers.

Usually, however, they just rest and sleep in the sun.

sea lion pup

Baby sea lions, called pups, are born on land. They start learning to swim when they are a few weeks old.

A Famous Sight

When California sea lions leave the water, they gather in large groups.

The most famous group of all can be found on PIER 39 in San Francisco.

People gather there every day to watch the sea lions.

Surprisingly, though, the animals didn't win fans by swimming at high speed or doing tricks.

They have become famous by just sitting on the dock and taking things slow.

PIER 39

HARASSMENT OF
SEA LIONS IS
A VIOLATION OF
THE MARINE
MAMMAL
PROTECTION ACT
• NO DOCKING

The California sea lions at PIER 39 are so popular that they have become known as "sea-lebrities."

Built for Speed

What makes a California sea lion swim so fast? Here is how different parts of the animal's body help it reach its amazing speeds.

back flippers help steer the body while swimming

body is streamlined, which means that water can pass over it easily—and not slow the sea lion down as it moves forward

head and neck also move to help steer the body

powerful front flippers move front to back to pull the sea lion through the water

Glossary

flippers (FLIP-urz) front and back limbs on a sea lion's body that help it move and steer

mammals (MAM-uhlz) animals that are warm-blooded, nurse their young with milk, and have hair or fur on their skin

porpoising (POR-puh-sing) the action that happens when a swimming sea lion jumps out of the water and dives back in

prey (PRAY) animals that are hunted for food

Index

Read More

Fetty, Margaret. *Sea Lions (Smart Animals!).* New York: Bearport (2007).

Johnson, Jinny. *Sea Lion.* North Mankato, MN: Smart Apple Media (2007).

Whitehouse, Patricia. *Sea Lion.* Chicago: Heinemann (2003).

Learn More Online

To learn more about sea lions, visit
www.bearportpublishing.com/BlinkofanEye

About the Author

Natalie Lunis has written many science and nature books for children. She lives in the Hudson River Valley, just north of New York City.